I0878689

INSPIRATIONS

pil
Publications International, Ltd.

Images from Shutterstock.com

Louis Weber, CEO
Publications International, Ltd.
8140 Lehigh Avenue
Morton Grove, IL 60053

ISBN: 978-1-63938-814-1

Manufactured in China.

8 7 6 5 4 3 2 1

TABLE OF CONTENTS

INTRODUCTION

I saw above a sea of hills
A solitary planet shine,
And there was no one, near or far,
To keep the world from being mine.

—Sara Teasdale

Life has many seasons: You may face times with more change than you feel prepared to handle or quiet periods in need of a spark. In this book, you'll discover a selection of uplifting ideas, poems, and quotes that encourage you to believe in yourself and take action to achieve your dreams.

Inspirations can be read from front to back, or you can turn to a section that resonates with your current aspirations. Reflect on passages that motivate you to reach new heights or appreciate what you have. During difficult times, you can find comfort in chapters on overcoming adversity and stress relief. Each of the ten chapters also shares several positive affirmations you can recite to boost self-confidence and challenge negative thinking.

Embrace life's journey wherever it takes you—or seize the reins and showcase your true potential.

PURSUE YOUR PURPOSE

There are many words of wisdom
Friends and teachers will impart,
But the wisest words of all will come
From deep within your heart.

So follow not the road well toiled,
Nor walk another's way,
But find the path that's yours alone
And boldly seize each day.

The quest for purpose is a journey without end, where every step invites you to reflect on and redefine your path. Face the journey with an open heart, knowing that it's never too late to discover new meaning.

The two most important days in life are the day you are born and the day you discover the reason why.

—Mark Twain

Ambition called to me,
but I dreaded the chances.
Yet all the while I hungered
for meaning in my life.
And now I know we must lift the sail
And catch the winds of destiny
Wherever they drive the boat.

—Edgar Lee Masters

Always be willing to push yourself in new directions. You may discover a destination you could not have imagined.

Success is a deeply personal journey, unique to the individual. Its meaning is as diverse as the people who seek it. The pursuit of success is not just about reaching goals; it's about embracing the journey and growing with the challenges along the way.

Before we set our hearts too much upon anything, let us examine how happy those are who already possess it.

—François de La Rochefoucauld

Affirmation

I will go where the energy makes my heart palpitate and spirit sing, for there I will find fulfillment.

Most of the time, life
whispers only soft clues,
gently suggesting the
path to follow.

Heed the whispers.
Learn the language.
Listen to yourself.

When you sit quietly
with your thoughts
and feelings, you can
find the path leading
to your purpose.

Just as every thread weaves into a rich tapestry, your unique gifts and perspective contribute depth to the fabric of your community. Embrace your individuality; variety allows the world to flourish.

There are loyal hearts,
there are spirits brave,
There are souls that
are pure and true;
Then give to the world
the best you have,
And the best will come back to you.

—Madeline S. Bridges

You are the captain of your ship,
the navigator of your destiny.

As you turn to face the future,
know that all you have learned in the past
will be your rudder, guiding your boat across
the vast sea of potential to the distant shore
where your next adventure awaits.

Seek comfort in the garden, seek adventure in the wilderness, but seek the truth within yourself.

The meaning I picked, the
one that most changed my life:
Overcome fear, behold wonder.

—Aeschylus

The mystery of human existence lies not in just staying alive, but in finding something to live for.

—Fyodor Dostoevsky

When you dedicate yourself to helping your community, you discover the profound impact of your actions. In that shared journey, a sense of meaning lights your path forward, making all around you richer and more vibrant.

Doing nothing for others is the undoing of one's self. We must be purposely kind and generous, or we miss the best part of existence.

The heart that goes out of itself gets large and full of joy. This is the great secret of inner life. We do ourselves the most good when we are doing something for others.

—Horace Mann

Teach others what you have learned, share the lessons of your life experience, and give freely from the store of knowledge within. All this will give your life meaning.

Affirmation

I will find the light that makes me shine and then use those rays to illuminate my way.

We live in deeds, not years;
in thoughts, not breaths;
In feelings, not in figures on a dial.
We should count time by
heart-throbs. He most lives
Who thinks most, feels the
noblest, acts the best.

—Philip James Bailey

Affirmation

In the trials I face throughout my life, I learn more about myself. I will embrace challenges as opportunities to nurture my personal growth and discover what is most valuable to me. Through hardship I can find meaning and renewal.

Our souls are like pools of still water upon which the rains of life fall, sending out tiny ripples that whisper our destiny's call.

The mind, after being confined at home for a while, sends the imagination abroad in quest of new treasures, and the body may as well accompany it.

—Hannah Webster Foster

There rises an unspeakable desire,
A longing to inquire
Into the mystery of this heart which beats
So wild, so deep in us, to know
Whence our lives come and where they go.

—Matthew Arnold

The purpose of life
is not to be happy. It is
to be useful, to be honorable,
to be compassionate, to have it
make some difference that you
have lived and lived well.

—Ralph Waldo Emerson

BELIEVE IN YOURSELF

When I rise up above the earth,
And look down on the things that fetter me,
I beat my wings upon the air,
Or tranquil lie,
Surge after surge of potent strength
Like incense comes to me.

—Georgia Douglas Johnson

Dare to be what you are,
and learn to resign with a good
grace all that you are not and to
believe in your own individuality.

—Henri-Frédéric Amiel

The moment you doubt
whether you can fly,
you cease forever
to be able to do it.

—J. M. Barrie

The future holds limitless
possibilities for all who
believe in themselves.

Every individual has
a place to fill in the world and is
important in some respect, whether
he chooses to be so or not.

—Nathaniel Hawthorne

How perfect the earth,
and the minutest thing upon it!
What is called good is perfect,
and what is called bad is just as perfect,
The vegetables and minerals are all perfect,
and the imponderable fluids perfect;
Slowly and surely they have pass'd on to
this, and slowly and surely they yet pass on.

—Walt Whitman

Affirmation

Today I am inspired to go beyond the boundaries of my weaknesses, challenge my limitations, and believe in endless possibilities.

You must do the thing
you think you cannot do.

—Eleanor Roosevelt

The sun shines not on us but in us.

—John Muir

Affirmation

I will not let the pessimists of the world squelch my belief that what I do can make a difference. I am determined to maintain my inspiration to change the world in whatever small ways I can.

At first people refuse to believe
that a strange new thing can be done,
then they begin to hope it can be done,
then they see it can be done—then it
is done and all the world wonders
why it was not done centuries ago.

—Frances Hodgson Burnett

Optimist: Person who travels on nothing from nowhere to happiness.

—Mark Twain

If you keep taking steps that move you forward, you will always be heading in the right direction.

One song can spark a moment,
One flower can wake the dream.
One tree can start a forest,
One bird can herald spring.

One smile begins a friendship,
One hand clasp lifts a soul.
One star can guide a ship at sea,
One word can frame the goal.

One vote can change a nation,
One sunbeam lights a room.
One candle wipes out darkness,
One laugh will conquer gloom.

Those who dream by day
are cognizant of many
things which escape those
who dream only by night.

—Edgar Allan Poe

It irritates me to be told how things have always been done. I defy the tyranny of precedent. I cannot afford the luxury of a closed mind.

—Clara Barton

I value not the censures
of the crowd.

—Aphra Behn

The more solitary,
the more friendless,
the more unsustained
I am, the more I will
respect myself.

—Charlotte Brontë

For she had come to feel that it was the only thing worth saying—what one felt. Cleverness was silly. One must say simply what one felt.

—Virginia Woolf

Nothing resembles selfishness more closely than self-respect.

—George Sand

By revealing the beauty of your inner self, you can help others find the path to confidence.

The creation of a thousand forests is in one acorn.

—Ralph Waldo Emerson

There is no ocean so wide
that someone can't sail it.
There is no mountain so tall
that someone can't scale it.
There is no task so arduous
that someone can't teach it.
There is no dream so impossible
that someone can't reach it.

Keep away from people who
try to belittle your ambitions.
Small people always do that,
but the really great make you feel
that you, too, can become great.

—Mark Twain

At times we may come across those who wish to darken our star instead of brightening their own.

They are free to make their choices, and we are free to stand tall and keep shining.

All greatness of character is dependent on individuality.

—James Fenimore Cooper

The most common form of despair is not being who you are.

—Søren Kierkegaard

Affirmation

When the winds of life blow,

I’ll hang onto myself.

When the road forks in two,

I’ll be true to myself.

When the going gets rough,

I’ll take care of myself.

When the journey gets long,

I’ll believe in myself.

Confidence does not always come naturally. Challenge negative thoughts and practice kind self-talk. With time, your confidence will grow.

I celebrate myself,
and sing myself,
And what I assume
you shall assume,
For every atom belonging to me
as good belongs to you.

—Walt Whitman

OVERCOME ADVERSITY

There's a pang in all rejoicing,
And a joy in the heart of pain;
And the wind that saddens,
the sea that gladdens,
Are singing the selfsame strain.

—Bayard Taylor

Storms sometimes arrive in our lives with hurricane-force winds. We feel as if our hearts are caught in the vortex. But just when we think we'll be destroyed, a small voice appears in the eye of the storm to remind us that we are not alone.

Look fear in the face and it will cease to trouble you.

There are some things
you learn best in calm,
and some in storm.

—Willa Cather

It is by surmounting difficulties, not by sinking under them, that we discover our fortitude. True courage consists not in flying from the storms of life, but in braving and steering through them with prudence.

—Hannah Webster Foster

Affirmation

I will no longer run from sorrow,
for I've discovered pain can inspire.
Many love songs and powerful poems
were forged in times of adversity.
I will learn how to sit with sadness
and allow it to pass through me.

It is good to embrace a hope.

—Ovid

See how time makes all grief decay.

—Adelaide Anne Procter

Affirmation

When fear insists I must run away, hope gives me the strength to stay.

Life, believe, is not a dream,
So dark as sages say;
Oft a little morning rain
Foretells a pleasant day.
Sometimes there are clouds of gloom,
But these are transient all;
If the shower will make the roses bloom,
O why lament its fall?

—Charlotte Brontë

No matter how alone you feel,
when you look to the left and
to the right, you will find your
journey is a shared one.

A little word in kindness spoken,
A motion or a tear,
Has often healed the heart that's broken
And made a friend sincere.

—Daniel Clement Colesworthy

The sun shines brighter
in the company of a friend.
Dark clouds float away, and
the road stretches beyond the
distant horizon. Adventures lie
before us that we would not
undertake alone. Friendship
carries us through trying times.

We cannot tell the precise moment when friendship is formed. As in filling a vessel drop by drop, there is at last a drop which makes it run over; so in a series of kindnesses there is at last one which makes the heart run over.

—Samuel Johnson

I will not allow my life's light to be determined by the darkness around me.

—Sojourner Truth

Happy are those who dare courageously to defend what they love.

—Ovid

Hope knows on the
other side of pain is joy;
on the other side of
injustice is peace.

When we experience loss, we have an opportunity to grow stronger. Loss enhances our appreciation for the given moment because it helps us understand the fleeting nature of all things. And feeling loss firsthand allows us to counsel others because we truly understand.

Affirmation

In times of loss and sorrow,
When my heart is dark with pain,
I will find a source of light within
To make life bright again.

A wise mind knows that adverse events are often opportunities for growth in disguise.

If we had no winter,
the spring would not
be so pleasant.
If we did not sometimes
taste of adversity,
prosperity would not
be so welcome.

—Anne Bradstreet

The gem cannot be polished without friction, nor man perfected without trials.

—Confucius

Life's tragedies make us into stepping stones. Without suffering, we would be like lumps of clay that have not yet been fired in the potter's oven to a transforming state of usefulness.

The fearful mind sees an obstacle and accepts it as a limitation that cannot be overcome. The inspired mind embraces that same obstacle as an opportunity for growth and a doorway into a realm of new possibilities.

Great emergencies and crises show us how much greater our vital resources are than we had supposed.

—William James

I have not failed.
I have discovered
twelve hundred materials
that don't work.

—Thomas Edison

I may not reach the heights I seek,
My untried strength may fail me;
Or, half-way up the mountain peak
Fierce tempests may assail me.
But though that place I never gain,
Herein lies comfort for my pain—
I will be worthy of it.

—Ella Wheeler Wilcox

When the anguish of loss overwhelms us
And we feel there's no reason to live,
We must look deep within to find meaning
And to know we've still so much to give.

There is no good reason
why we should fear the future,
but there is every reason why
we should face it seriously,
neither hiding from ourselves
the gravity of the problems
before us nor fearing to
approach these problems with
the unbending, unflinching
purpose to solve them aright.

—Theodore Roosevelt

EMBRACE CHANGE

Life's rarest moments
are derived from change.
The heart outgrows
old happiness, old grief,
And suns itself in feelings
new and strange.
The most enduring pleasure
is but brief.

—Ella Wheeler Wilcox

Affirmation

I will not fear change but know that all change is simply the way of moving my life forward in the direction of my destiny.

A great change in life is like a cold bath in winter—we all hesitate at the first plunge.

—Letitia Elizabeth Landon

Weary the cloud falleth
out of the sky,
Dreary the leaf lieth low.
All things must come
to the earth by and by,
Out of which all things grow.

—Owen Meredith

Imagine a tree that
refused to shed its dead leaves.
Where would the new leaves find
room to bloom forth in abundance?
By trimming the old, we make way
for new growth.

Human nature will not flourish, any more than a potato, if it be planted and replanted, for too long a series of generations, in the same worn-out soil.

—Nathaniel Hawthorne

Take time to pull weeds and plant new seeds—then enjoy the garden you created.

The real voyage of discovery
lies not in seeking new landscapes
but in having new eyes.

—Marcel Proust

Affirmation

I will cultivate enthusiasm, for it brings new life into old tasks and joy into dull situations. Sometimes I cannot change the world around me, but I can change my perspective.

Change is never easy, but the gifts it bestows are magnificent. Just imagine the caterpillar struggling within the confines of a cocoon. Even as it struggles, it is becoming something glorious and beautiful, soon to emerge as a winged butterfly.

Change may bring temporary pain and discomfort, but it also brings the promise of a new life filled with joy and the ability to soar even higher than you ever did before.

Weep not that the
world changes—did it keep
A stable, changeless state,
'twere cause indeed to weep.

—William Cullen Bryant

There is pleasure in new friendships, comfort in old ones, and sweet memories to treasure in those we've lost.

We pass through seasons in friendships, just as we pass through seasons of the year. Our relationships with others grow, bloom, and sometimes wilt, merely because the time has come. We don't need to regret these natural passings. Instead, we can look at the past with fondness, knowing that spring will soon come.

But the nearer the dawn
the darker the night,
And by going wrong
all things come right;
Things have been mended
that were worse,
And the worse, the nearer
they are to mend.

—Henry Wadsworth
Longfellow

There is in the worst
of fortune the best chances
for a happy change.

—Euripides

To-morrow to fresh woods,
and pastures new.

—John Milton

Affirmation

My body and mind are built for change. Sitting for too long in one position hurts—my joints and muscles crave movement. Just as it is healthy to move my body, it is healthy to stretch my mind. And with strenuous movement, my strength grows.

Do we fear suffering
or apathy most?
Is it from experience
or the monotony of a
commonplace existence
that we quickest flee?

—Anna Katharine Green

For just as the harshest winter always gives way to the warm blush of spring, the season of our suffering will give way to a brighter tomorrow, where change becomes a catalyst for new growth and maturity, and we are able to move on with the joyfulness of being alive.

You cannot step twice
into the same rivers;
for fresh waters are ever
flowing in upon you.

—Heraclitus

The old woman I shall become will be quite different from the woman I am now. Another I is beginning.

—George Sand

One by one
the sands are flowing,
One by one
the moments fall;
Some are coming,
some are going;
Do not strive
to grasp them all.

—Adelaide Anne Procter

When poised at the brink of a new beginning, you can either find a ladder to climb or learn to fly.

Resilience: An ability
to recover from or adjust
to misfortune or change.

Affirmation

I am resilient.
I have an unwavering
spirit that turns setbacks
into comebacks and
gives me the courage
to keep moving forward.

One doesn't discover new lands without consenting to lose sight of the shore for a very long time.

—André Gide

As wave is driven by wave
And each, pursued, pursues the wave ahead,
So time flies on and follows, flies, and follows,
Always, for ever and new. What was before
Is left behind; what never was is now;
And every passing moment is renewed.

—Ovid

RELIEVE STRESS

Between me and the noise of strife
Are walls of mountains set with pine;
The dusty, care-strewn paths of life
Lead not to this retreat of mine.

—Alexander Posey

In the solitude of a natural setting,
the heart discovers serenity,
the soul knows abiding peace,
and the spirit finds renewal.

I go to nature to be soothed
and healed, and to have
my senses put in order.

—John Burroughs

Affirmation

I will not dwell too long on
what was or what might have been;
what will be is waiting.

Travel light. If you must carry baggage, make sure it's neatly packed and portable. Leave behind anything too bulky or too painful to carry easily.

A thing of beauty is a joy for ever;
Its loveliness increases; it will never
Pass into nothingness; but still will keep
A bower quiet for us, and a sleep
Full of sweet dreams, and health,
and quiet breathing.

—John Keats

A small thing, as simple
as a breath of fresh air,
supports the changes we make.
The present is breathing in,
and the past is exhalation.

Take rest; a field that has rested gives a beautiful crop.

—Ovid

You must sit down and soothe your weary body precisely when you have no time to do so.

Rest is not idleness,
and to lie sometimes
on the grass under the
trees on a summer's day,
listening to the murmur
of water, or watching the
clouds float across the
blue sky, is by no means
a waste of time.

—Sir John Lubbock

The true harvest of my daily life is somewhat as intangible and indescribable as the tints of morning or evening. It is a little star dust caught, a segment of the rainbow which I have clutched.

—Henry David Thoreau

Affirmation

I can decide to be at peace
with the state of my life.
I can pause the constant desire
for more and better things.
I am content with what I have,
and that is true peace.

There is no remedy
so easy as books, which if
they do not give cheerfulness,
at least restore quiet to the
most troubled mind.

—Mary Wortley Montagu

That perfect tranquility of life, which is nowhere to be found but in retreat, a faithful friend, and a good library.

—Aphra Behn

When our lives are overloaded, one of the first joys we cut back on is the time we spend with our friends. But it is those very relationships that help center us, calm our worries, and remind us of our true priorities.

The true way to soften one's troubles is to solace those of others.

—Françoise d'Aubigné

Geese take turns,
take up the slack, in the
natural rhythm of flight.

By sharing our journey,
we too gain that updraft
of air where we rest
awhile, knowing love is
under our wings.

Affirmation

I am open to asking for help when I need it. In times of stress, I am worthy of support. My connections to friends, loved ones, and the world around me are a source of strength.

When we struggle
in the search for harmony,
we need only remember to
look to nature for the answer.

Nothing thrills the heart and awakens the spirit like a thunderstorm. Without a reminder of our deep connection to the natural world, we can grow dull and lifeless, stiff and anxious, lost and uncertain. Then the thunder roars and the lightning pierces the dark sky, and we remember we are part of something infinite and sublime.

Worry and fear are robbers, taking from us those things that are not yet missing.

Thousands of tired,
nerve-shaken, over-civilized
people are beginning to
find out that going to the
mountains is going home;
that wildness is a necessity;
and that mountain parks
and reservations are useful
not only as fountains of
timber and irrigating rivers,
but as fountains of life.

—John Muir

When feeling inadequate or overwhelmed, consider that the forest would be silent if the birds sang only the songs they had perfected.

Nature, time, and patience are the three great physicians.

—H. G. Bohn

Sometimes—ofttimes—I almost feel
The calm upon my senses steal,
So soft, and all but hear
The dead leaves rustle near
And sign to be
At rest with me.

—Alexander Posey

Embrace simplicity.

—Lao-tzu

FOSTER INNER PEACE

Peace flows into me
As the tide to the pool by the shore;
It is mine forevermore,
It will not ebb like the sea.

—Sara Teasdale

The greatest weapon against stress is our ability to choose one thought over another.

—William James

Affirmation

I release what I cannot control
and focus on what I can change.
By letting go,
I invite tranquility into my life.

Let mystery have its place in you; do not be always turning up your whole soil with the plowshare of self-examination, but leave a little fallow corner in your heart ready for any seed the winds may bring, and reserve a nook of shadow for the passing bird.

—Henri-Frédéric Amiel

Don't seek peace and
tranquility from outside sources;
they reside within your own heart.

The lure of the distant and the difficult is deceptive. The great opportunity is where you are.

—John Burroughs

The wise know that
a journey is meaningless
without occasionally stopping
to enjoy the view.

When you are waiting for a train,
don't keep perpetually looking to see
if it is coming. The time of its arrival is
the business of the conductor, not yours.

—Anna Brackett

It is a great thing to know
the season for speech
and the season for silence.

—Seneca

Life seems but a quick
succession of busy nothings.

—Jane Austen

Blocks of time to yourself can be difficult to come by. Learn to snatch it in tidbits: a solitary cup of coffee, a peaceful stroll at lunch, an extra-long shower.

Affirmation

I am deserving of rest and serenity, and I can create space for calm in my life. By honoring my needs, I can face the world and the needs of those I care about with a healthier spirit.

Fear no more, says the heart,
committing its burden to some sea,
which sighs collectively for all sorrows,
and renews, begins, collects, lets fall.

—Virginia Woolf

Find your place in the sun.

Then take a nap.

When we fill our days with the noisy blur of constant activity, we miss the insights found in stillness. It is only by purposely taking time to sit silently that we cultivate wisdom. In quiet and solitude, we can renew our connection to our inner sources of inspiration, energy, and enthusiasm.

I do not ask for any crown
But that which all may win;
Nor try to conquer the world
Except the one within.

—Louisa May Alcott

Climb the mountains and get their good tidings. Nature's peace will flow into you as sunshine flows into trees. The winds will blow their own freshness into you, and the storms their energy, while cares will drop away from you like the leaves of Autumn.

—John Muir

Living in harmony with nature's seasons awakens us to spring's lush renewal, fall's cozy slowness, winter's savory rest, and summer's exuberance. Thus we are reminded to honor each season's energy for the wisdom it holds.

I like trees because they seem
more resigned to the way they
have to live than other things do.
I feel as if this tree knows everything
I ever think of when I sit here.
When I come back to it, I never
have to remind it of anything;
I begin just where I left off.

—Willa Cather

Throughout our lives, patience is a virtue many find difficult to practice. The slow and seasonal workings of nature can provide the perfect inspiration.

Anger robs us of our peace. It affects our minds, our bodies, and our emotions. If we choose to let go of anger, we can embrace peace again.

Affirmation

I release anger that does not serve me. Although anger can drive meaningful action or self-protection, I will not let it overstay. I will be at ease with myself and others, cultivating compassion and forgiveness.

If you look the right way,

you can see the whole world is a garden.

—Frances Hodgson Burnett

Sometime in the hazy morning between "waking up" and "not yet," take the time to listen to your own soul.

Sweet Solitude!
I love thy silent shade,
I love to pause
when in life's mad career;
To view the chequered path
before me laid,
And turn to meditate—
to hope, to fear.

'Tis sweet to draw
the curtain on the world,
To shut out all its tumult, all its care;
Leave the dread vortex,
in which all are whirled,
And to thy shades
of twilight calm repair.

—Lucretia Maria Davidson

A happy life consists
in tranquility of the mind.

—Cicero

NURTURE GRATITUDE

With a grateful heart,
I appreciate what is.

Every challenge brings
the gift of wisdom.
Every obstacle strengthens
my unbreaking resolve.
Every abundance gives me
more to share with others.
Every sorrow resolves
into joy tomorrow.

Guard well within yourself that treasure, kindness. Know how to give without hesitation, how to lose without regret, how to acquire without meanness.

—George Sand

Gratitude is an attitude of loving what you have, and this undoubtedly leads to having even more.

Let us be grateful to the people who make us happy; they are the charming gardeners who make our souls blossom.

—Marcel Proust

In the garden of life,
even the lowliest weed serves a purpose, if only to remind us just how beautiful the flowers are.

I learned to look more upon the bright side of my condition, and less upon the dark side, and to consider what I enjoyed rather than what I wanted; and this gave me sometimes such secret comforts, that I cannot express them.

—Daniel Defoe

Affirmation

I am grateful for the people and comforts around me. Through quiet reflection, I appreciate the wonders of life and find inspiration in the present moment.

Then do not grasp at
the stars, but do life's plain,
common work as it comes,
certain that daily duties
and daily bread are the
sweetest things in life.

—Robert Louis Stevenson

I have nature and art
and poetry, and if that is not
enough, what is enough?

—Vincent van Gogh

Because we live in a fast-paced society, it is easy to feel fragmented. We may skim over the surface of projects or relationships in order to "save time."

May we not be spread so thin that we fail to appreciate the nuances of our work, our home, and the people we love. Let us resist taking the shallow route and instead pursue depth in our lives.

Affirmation

I can create the space
to slow down and cherish
the good things in my life.
Each day, I have at least one
gift for which to be grateful:
watching the sun rise
on a new morning.

Do not spoil what you have by desiring what you have not; remember that what you now have was once among the things you only hoped for.

—Epicurus

To study hard, think quietly, talk gently,
act frankly, to listen to stars, birds,
babes, and sages with open heart,
to bear all cheerfully, do all bravely,
await occasions, hurry never…
This is to be my symphony.

—William Henry Channing

It is unnecessary to heighten the glory of day by comparing it with the preceding twilight.

—Catharine Maria Sedgwick

May we always be grateful
For guiding lights along the way,
For all the mentors who shaped us
Into the people we are today.

Love takes many forms,
each with its own qualities.
Value and appreciate each
one for the special joy it
brings to your life.

We are like islands in the sea,
separate on the surface
but connected in the deep.

—William James

Seize time with growing children and aging loved ones—as much for your sake as theirs.

Affirmation

I am loved and give love in return.
My thoughtful words and actions radiate through the lives of those around me.
Through gratitude I can access a deep kindness that uplifts and inspires, spreading love to all.

This world... wonderful, inscrutable, magical, and more, to whosoever will think of it.

—Thomas Carlyle

I am larger, better than I thought,
I did not know I held so much goodness.

All seems beautiful to me,
I can repeat over to men and women
You have done such good to me
I would do the same to you...
I will toss a new gladness
and roughness among them,
Whoever denies me it shall not trouble me,
Whoever accepts me he or she
shall be blessed and shall bless me.

—Walt Whitman

If Nature has made you for a giver, your hands are born open, and so is your heart; and though there may be times when your hands are empty, your heart is always full, and you can give things out of that—warm things, kind things, sweet things—help and comfort and laughter.

—Frances Hodgson Burnett

Flowers are lovely;

Love is flower-like;

Friendship is a sheltering tree.

—Samuel Taylor Coleridge

It was the touch of the imperfect upon the would-be perfect that gave the sweetness, because it was that which gave the humanity.

—Thomas Hardy

Gifts are always found in lessons.
Recognize when adversity is followed
by hope, healing, and newfound joy.
Be grateful for challenges that stretch
you beyond your comfort zone.
Give thanks for difficult times that make
you appreciate the good times more.
Live with gratitude for the diverse
experiences life provides.

FIND HAPPINESS

I will be the gladdest thing
Under the sun!
I will touch a hundred flowers
And not pick one.

—Edna St. Vincent Millay

An optimistic outlook may not speed the journey, but it does improve the scenery along the way.

Thus happiness depends,
as Nature shows,
Less on exterior things
than most suppose.

—William Cowper

Find something you love to do and throw yourself into it wholeheartedly. Minds were designed to implement the heart's desires.

Affirmation

I will pour my heart into what I love,
creating beauty and joy in every endeavor.
By dedicating myself to my passions,
I both discover and spread happiness.

A beautiful view.
A mouthwatering meal.
A movie that inspires or a project completed.
When we share our pleasures or projects, we bond with others, create meaning, and enjoy working toward a common goal. Shared pleasures enhance life.

The best way to cheer yourself is to try to cheer somebody else up.

—Mark Twain

Life is short and we have never too much time for gladdening the hearts of those who are travelling the dark journey with us. Oh be swift to love, make haste to be kind.

—Henri-Frédéric Amiel

Friends are good for us. Friendships with depth and meaning validate our sense of self and strengthen our identity as someone who matters. Old friendships draw on our years of shared experiences, providing comfort. With the help of friends, we weather loss and celebrate joy.

One is happy once one knows the necessary ingredients of happiness: simple tastes, a certain degree of courage, self-denial to a point, love of work, and above all, a clear conscience.

—George Sand

If I have my friends,

I have all the wealth I desire.

If I have my family,

I have all the love I want.

If I have my self-respect,

I have all the confidence I require.

If I have my health,

I have all the power I need.

All good things
are wild and free.

—Henry David Thoreau

Affirmation

I will dance when I feel the urge.

I will sing loudly when I sing.

I will stand in awe when I catch a glimpse of something wondrous.

I will not hide my joy.

To a great experience one thing is essential—an experiencing nature.

—Walter Bagehot

He was mastered by the sheer surging of life, the tidal wave of being, the perfect joy of each separate muscle, joint, and sinew in that it was everything that was not death, that it was aglow and rampant, expressing itself in movement, flying exultantly under the stars.

—Jack London

Lie on your back in the freshly cut grass and count stars in the inky sky, knowing there is much of life yet to discover and enjoy.

When you are in the midst of suffering, time is too slow. When you are in the midst of excitement, time moves too quickly. Only in the present moment does time cease to exist. True happiness is found there, in the now, where regrets of the past and the fears of the future give way to the bliss of just being alive.

In the human heart new passions are forever being born; the overthrow of one almost always means the rise of another.

—François de La Rochefoucauld

There's a place of renewal and happiness within you. All you need to do to reach it is withdraw your attention from the outside world and focus on the strength and the energy inside yourself.

Hopeful people have a peace about them,
a way of looking at everything that happens
as an opportunity for growth and happiness.
While their lives may not be any easier,
their attitude sets them apart.

Affirmation

I am strong enough to carry hope. I will not undercut myself, my happiness, or my dreams but instead approach life's journey with a positive mindset, confident that good things are always on the horizon.

Happiness is like a butterfly which, when pursued, is always beyond our grasp, but, if you will sit down quietly, may alight upon you.

—Nathaniel Hawthorne

Seek out those things that
make your soul sing.

There's a flower at my window in full bloom.
It is radiant in the sunshine,
and so cheerful after rain;
And it wafts upon the air its sweet perfume.

—Lucian B. Watkins

Happy is the person who knows that life's greatest treasures are often buried deep within the simplest things, waiting to be discovered by those who are paying attention.

SPARK CREATIVITY

From mind alone
springs shapes so clear,
A vision only the heart can steer,
Ink and color, imagined place,
Crafting worlds from
empty space.

Passion is the genesis of genius.

—Galileo Galilei

The poetry of the earth
is never dead.

—John Keats

As long as I live, I'll hear waterfalls and birds and winds sing. I'll interpret the rocks, learn the language of flood, storm and the avalanche. I'll acquaint myself with the glaciers and wild gardens, and get as near the heart of the world as I can.

—John Muir

There are two kinds of artists in this world; those that work because the spirit is in them, and they cannot be silent if they would, and those that speak from a conscientious desire to make apparent to others the beauty that has awakened their own admiration.

—Anna Katharine Green

Affirmation

My artistic endeavors are a radiant testament to my unique spirit and creativity. I will embrace my gifts and let my inner self shine.

Nothing great was ever accomplished by sticking to the status quo. In order to experience life fully, you must roll up your sleeves and risk facing a blank canvas or making a few creative mistakes. But at least you will have tried, dared, dreamed.

A wise person doesn't
batter against stone walls
but finds a way around them,
under them, or over them.

Whoever wants to tell
a variety of stories ought to
have a variety of beginnings.

—Marie de France

The more energy, creativity, and enthusiasm we put into the time we've been given, the more we'll get back in the form of new experiences and opportunities for a fulfilling life.

Art is the most intense mode of individualism that the world has known.

—Oscar Wilde

Where there is no novelty,
there can be no curiosity.

—Aphra Behn

It is better to fail in originality
than to succeed in imitation.

—Herman Melville

Creative people don't have
more ideas than other people.
They have merely learned
to recognize them.

Affirmation

I find inspiration in everyday moments and use it to fuel my creative endeavors. I will trust the process, knowing my ideas will flow so long as I commit to setting pen to paper, notes to music, brushstrokes to canvas.

And moreover, to succeed, the artist must possess the courageous soul. The brave soul. The soul that dares and defies.

—Kate Chopin

My heart must find vent at my pen.

—Abigail Adams

Art is unquestionably one of the purest and highest elements in human happiness. It trains the mind through the eye, and the eye through the mind. As the sun colors flowers, so does art color life.

—Sir John Lubbock

Only through art can
we get outside ourselves
and know another's view
of the universe.

—Marcel Proust

The creative spark catches fire in the soul, and we are warmed by the flush of inspiration.

Affirmation

Today belongs to me.
It's a clean page I can
cover with my vision.
I welcome fresh and
innovative thoughts with
excitement and curiosity.

Life seems to go on without effort when I am filled with music.

—George Eliot

Music is the soul's celebration of life.

Some beautiful things are more impressive when left imperfect than when too highly finished.

—François de La Rochefoucauld

When we daydream, we look to the future and the past. Our creativity gets a jump start, and sometimes the solution to a seemingly insolvable problem becomes clear. Honoring the time to reflect helps us stay in tune with what is important to us. May we always make time to dip into ourselves and dream.

Her secret? It is every artist's secret... passion. That is all. It is an open secret, and perfectly safe. Like heroism, it is inimitable in cheap materials.

—Willa Cather

What is art,
But life upon the larger scale, the higher,
When, graduating up in a spiral line
Of still expanding and ascending gyres,
It pushes toward the intense significance
Of all things, hungry for the Infinite?

—Elizabeth Barrett Browning

The artist is nothing without the gift, but the gift is nothing without work.

—Émile Zola

ACHIEVE YOUR DREAMS

A gentle tug of the heartstrings,
An urging from deep within,
The whisper of sweet inspiration
Is how all great achievements begin.

Feel the power of living
in hope, for it is that place
in the heart that lies between
dreaming and doing.

If a little dreaming is dangerous, the cure for it is not to dream less, but to dream more, to dream all the time.

—Marcel Proust

When you let a goal enter
your heart as well as your mind,
it becomes twice as obtainable.

Affirmation

I will step into the future with my eyes clearly focused on my dreams. I will not let day-to-day life distract me from my grander goals.

Far away there
in the sunshine are
my highest aspirations.
I may not reach them,
but I can look up and
see their beauty, believe
in them, and try to follow
where they lead.

—Louisa May Alcott

Beginning each day as if something good will happen moves us further toward that possibility. Doubt, however, seldom takes the first step.

When your dreams seem unreachable, trust that the future will lighten your burdens, smooth your path, and urge you on to a brighter tomorrow.

Far better it is to dare
mighty things, to win
glorious triumphs,
even though checkered
by failure, than to take
rank with those poor
spirits who neither enjoy
much nor suffer much,
because they live in the
gray twilight that knows
not victory nor defeat.

—Theodore Roosevelt

Progress may not always require continuing forward on the same path. It may mean retracing your steps, taking an unexpected turn, or even stopping to rest and renew your spirit.

Rather, ten times, die in the surf, heralding the way to a new world, than stand idly on the shore.

—Florence Nightingale

Success comes to those who have proceeded to do what the rest of us have always intended to do.

Affirmation

I am confident in my abilities.
I can turn my dreams into goals,
make a plan to achieve them, and
follow that plan to a brighter future.

If we take care of the moments, the years will take care of themselves.

—Maria Edgeworth

Do not look back and agonize over roads not taken, dreams not pursued. Instead, look ahead to the future with new roads to discover and dreams to fulfill.

Dripping water hollows
out stone, not through force
but through persistence.

—Ovid

If one advances
confidently in the direction
of his dreams, and
endeavors to live the life
which he has imagined,
he will meet with a
success unexpected in
common hours.

—Henry David Thoreau

It's easy to become discouraged when we can see little progress being made toward our goals. Although it may look as if nothing is happening, remember that the surface of a pond often appears still and quiet, but there is ever-abundant activity going on just below.

I attribute my success to this:
I never gave or took an excuse.

—Florence Nightingale

When broken dreams cross my path,
it helps to know that it takes broken soil to
grow a flower, broken clouds to bring rain,
and broken grain to make bread.

Hope is like the sun, which,
as we journey towards it, casts the
shadow of our burden behind us.

—Samuel Smiles

The song of the universe is
sung through each one of us.
Its notes, our dreams and visions;
its melody, how far we've come.

Affirmation

On my quest to capture my dreams, I will never fear mistakes, always share my lessons, and remember to smile at the world.

Destiny is not a matter of chance,
it is a matter of choice;
it is not a thing to be waited for,
it is a thing to be achieved.

—William Jennings Bryan

It will never rain roses:
when we want to have more roses,
we must plant more roses.

—George Eliot

There is no chance,
no destiny, no fate,
Can circumvent or
hinder or control
The firm resolve of
a determined soul.

—Ella Wheeler Wilcox